Awesome JOKES

Charles Keller
Illustrated by Jeff Sinclair

Sterling Publishing Co., Inc.   New York

To Gabriel

Library of Congress Cataloging-in-Publication Data Available

20   19   18

First paperback edition published in 1997 by
Sterling Publishing Co., Inc.
387 Park Avenue South, New York, NY 10016
© 1996 by Charles Keller
Distributed in Canada by Sterling Publishing
c/o Canadian Manda Group, 165 Dufferin Street
Toronto, Ontario, Canada M6K 3H6
Distributed in Great Britain and Europe by Chris Lloyd at Orca Book
Services, Stanley House, Fleets Lane, Poole BH15 3AJ, England
Distributed in Australia by Capricorn Link (Australia) Pty. Ltd.
P.O. Box 704, Windsor, NSW 2756, Australia

Printed in China
All rights reserved

Sterling ISBN 0-8069-4377-7 Hardcover
ISBN 0-8069-4378-5 Paperback

For information about custom editions, special sales, premium and
corporate purchases, please contact Sterling Special Sales
Department at 800-805-5489 or specialsales@sterlingpub.com.

Contents

1. Ask a Silly Question ...

What does a frog say when it sees something terrific?

"Toadally awesome!"

Why are frogs happy?

They get to eat what bugs them.

A snail was mugged by two turtles. He went to the police station to report the crime.

"Tell me exactly what happened," the police said.

"I can't," said the snail. "It all happened so fast."

Attacked by two muggers, a man tried to defend himself. He fought and fought and finally gave up. The muggers found 85 cents on him.

"You fought that hard for 85 cents?" asked the muggers.

"Gee," said the man, "I thought you were after the $500 I have in my shoe."

News bulletin: The crook who robbed the laundromat made a clean getaway.

What happens when you don't dust your mirror?
You get a dirty look.

How do you know when it's time to clean your room?
When you have to use a compass to find your bed.

MOTHER: You look pretty dirty, son.
SON: Gee, Mom, I think I look a lot better clean.

"Let me guess what you had for dinner last night. Meatballs and spaghetti, right?"

"Wow, that's amazing! Did you read my mind?"

"No, your chin."

What kind of thinking makes you the most tired?
Wrestling with your conscience.

WARPED WISE MAN SAYS

Water is a colorless liquid that turns black when you put your hands in it.

What's the best way to paint the ocean?
In watercolors.

What do you use to cut through the ocean waves?
A sea-saw.

"Son, if you want to learn anything you have to start at the bottom."
"But, Dad, I want to learn to swim."

"You shouldn't swim on an empty stomach."
"Okay, I'll swim on my back."

"It's great to be back from vacation. It rained the whole time."
"It couldn't have been that bad. You got a great tan."
"This isn't tan—it's rust."

What's brown, hairy and wears sunglasses?
A coconut on vacation.

What's a lumberjack's favorite month?
Sep-timber.

What was the sad evergreen doing?
Pining away.

Why did the tree fall asleep in the lumberyard?
It became bored.

What's a tree's favorite drink?
Root beer.

"Did you hear about the camper who bought a new sleeping bag?"
"No, what happened?"
"He spent two weeks trying to wake it up."

CAMPER: Can you pitch a tent?
BEGINNER: Overhand or underhand?

Did you hear about the hunter who came out of the woods and felt bushed?

DAFFYNITIONS

Polka—what you do to your sister when she falls asleep in church.

Thongs—what Tinatra sings.

Electrocute—shockingly good-looking.

Fireproof—the boss's son.

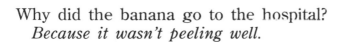

Why did the banana go to the hospital?
Because it wasn't peeling well.

"Stop worrying so much," said the doctor to the nervous patient. "Throw yourself into your work."
"But, Doc, I mix concrete for a living!"

"Doctor, Doctor, my brother thinks he's a quarter."
"Well, bring him in. I think I can change him."

"I have a problem. My doctor told me to take these pills for my insomnia, but I haven't taken any yet."

"Why not?"

"Because he told me to take them before going to sleep."

Why do teachers take aspirin?
For detention headaches.

What kind of headache does a hammer get?
Pounding ones.

What cheese does a cow like?
Moo-zzarella.

"We have a difficult life. There are two hundred cows on my father's farm and every morning my two brothers and I have to divvy up the milking chores."

"Wow! That sounds like exhausting work!"

"Well, it's better now that Dad bought 100 more cows."

"How can it be better with more cows to milk?"

"Hey, any fool can divide 300 by 3."

Did you hear the joke about the cows? It's udder nonsense.

What did the mama cow say to the baby cow?
"It's pasture bedtime."

Why did the horse put on the blanket?
He was a little colt.

What's a pig's favorite tale?
"Slopping Beauty."

TEACHER: What's a metaphor?
STUDENT: That's where sheep go to eat grass.

TEACHER: What are the last words of "The Star
    Spangled Banner"?
STUDENT: "Play Ball."

"I asked my mother for a new pair of sneakers
for gym."
    "What did she say?"
    "She said to tell Jim to buy his own
sneakers."

TOM SWIFTIES

"Is the lettuce fresh?" said Tom crisply.

"It's a dogs's life," Tom muttered.

"I'll never pet a lion again," said Tom offhandedly.

"I'm going to complain to the waiter about this hamburger," Tom beefed.

"Look at this twig," Tom snapped.

Why did the hamburger look sad?
Because it's grounded beef.

What do spiders eat with their hamburgers?
French flies.

What's a librarian's favorite food?
Shush-kebab.

CUSTOMER: Do you serve crabs here?
WAITER: We serve everybody. Have a seat.

DINER: I'll have what the man at the next table is having.

WAITER: Okay, but I don't think he'll be too happy about it.

"This restaurant has great food. I ordered a fresh egg and got the freshest egg in the world. I ordered a cup of hot coffee and got the hottest coffee in the world."

"Yes, I know. I ordered a small steak."

Where does a rabbit go when it needs grooming?

To the hare dresser.

Where do Easter bunnies dance?

At the basket ball.

LET'S GO TO THE *HOP!!..*

What's big, grey, floppy and goes Hoppity, BOOM, hoppity, BOOM?
The Easter Elephant.

What do you get if you cross a gopher with a porcupine?
A leaky tunnel.

That joke was as funny as a porcupine in a balloon factory.

Who lives underground and loves to paint?
Vincent Van Gopher.

How did the mouse lose its tail?
Catnip.

Why couldn't the writer cross the road?
He had authoritis.

"My dad drives like lightning."
"You mean he drives fast?"
"No, he strikes trees."

"Why are you crying?"
"My bowling ball is broken."
"How do you know?"
"It has holes in it."

2. Dork Ages

How many controls do you have on your TV set?
Four—my father, my mother and my two brothers.

BIFF: Do you have a family tree?
CLIFF: No, we don't even have a flower pot.

JO: I have a new baby brother.
FLO: What's his name?
JO: He won't tell me.

"Dad, there's a man at the door asking for you."
"With a bill?"
"No, with a nose just like yours."

What class does soda pop go to?
Fizz-ed.

What animal lives in a gym?
A gympanzee.

What would you get if you crossed a lobster
with a baseball player?
A pinch hitter.

Why does Cinderella like to play catch?
Because it's one ball after another.

WILLIE: I just found a lost baseball.
DAD: How do you know it was lost?
WILLIE: Because the kids down the street are
looking all over for it.

What two animals like to play baseball?
Bats and balled eagles.

Two baseball players, Ben and Ken, were talking. Ben said, "I wonder if there is baseball in heaven."

A short while later, Ken died. One day he appeared to Ben and said: "I've got good news and bad news. The good news is that there is baseball in heaven. The bad news is that you're pitching on Wednesday."

"Wow, it's a run home!"

"You mean a home run."

"No, I mean a run home. I just hit the ball through the neighbor's window."

WARPED WISE MAN SAYS

The trouble with being a good sport is that you have to lose to prove it.

What do you call a bunch of toads stacked on top of each other?
A toadem pole.

Show me a frog's favorite drink and I'll show you a Croak-a-Cola.

TEACHER: Henry Hudson was a famous explorer. He found the Hudson River.
STUDENT: Boy, that's some coincidence!

Why was Columbus a crook?
He double-crossed the Atlantic.

What do you call a rotten essay?
A decomposition.

TEACHER; This is the worst homework you've ever done, Jane.
JANE: So, now you can't even trust your parents.

TEACHER: Why didn't you do your homework?
PUPIL: My mother said I shouldn't do anything until I clean up my room.

MOTHER: The hardest assignment I ever had was to write an essay on the belly of a frog.
DAUGHTER: Wow, how'd you get the frog in the typewriter?

Did you hear the joke about the pair of cats?
It's a tale of two kitties.

What is the longest line at a joker's party?
The punch line.

What kind of jokes do vegetables like?
Corny ones.

Why did the bacon laugh?
One of the eggs cracked a yolk.

"Which came first the chicken or the egg?"
"The egg."
"Are you sure?"
"Yes, I had an egg for breakfast and I'm having chicken for lunch."

How does a comedian like his eggs?
Funny side up.

A fellow walked into a diner and ordered breakfast. "I want two eggs, one of them runny as water and the other cooked so hard you can bounce it off the wall. I want the toast burned black as coal and the coffee cold and the butter too hard to cut."

"We can't do that," replied the waiter.

"Why not?" asked the customer. "You did it yesterday."

"How many skinny people does it take to fill a bathtub?"

"I don't know—they keep slipping down the drain."

NAN: You've been counting calories for months now and you haven't lost any weight.

JAN: Yes, but my arithmetic is much better.

"I'm afraid you're going to have to diet," said the doctor, pointing to the man's belly.

"All right. But what color?"

Did you hear about the fellow who went on a diet, eating only dehydrated foods? One day he got caught in the rain and gained fifty pounds.

A woman with a weight problem went to see a doctor. The doctor put her on a diet.

"I want you to eat normally for a day and then skip a day. Repeat this procedure for two weeks and then come back to see me."

When she returned the doctor was delighted at her rapid weight loss. "You look great! Did you do this just by following my instructions?"

The woman nodded. "I'll tell you I didn't think I would make it. I thought I would faint."

"From hunger?" asked the doctor.

"No, from all that skipping," said the woman.

Thinking he was clever, a counterfeiter took a $1,000 bill to the bank.

"I'd like to exchange this for smaller bills," said the counterfeiter.

"Of course," replied the teller. "Would you like it in $200 or $300 bills?"

"I hear the bank is looking for a new teller."
"I thought they hired one a month ago."
"That's the one they're looking for."

PRISONER: Why are you in jail?
SECOND PRISONER: Well, I was making big money—about a half an inch too big.

What metal can't feel anything?
Aluminumb.

What cup can't you drink from?
A hiccup.

BOSS: Before I hire you, young man. I must tell you that this job requires someone who is responsible.

YOUNG MAN: Oh, that's me, all right. Everywhere I worked, when something went wrong, I was responsible.

BOSS: Did you mark the crate "Fragile, This Side Up"?

WORKER: Yes, sir, and just to be safe, I marked it that way on both sides.

BOSS: Didn't you get the letter that said you were fired?

EX-EMPLOYEE: Yes sir, but on the envelope it said, "Return after five days." So here I am.

Why was the man fired from the M & M factory?
He threw away all the W's.

"I sold my dog for $1,000."
"That's great. What did you do with all that money?"
"Oh, I didn't get any money. I got two $500 cats."

What kind of cat likes to go bowling?
An alley cat.

Where do cats go to dance?
To the fur ball.

What do you call a plump cat that swallows a duck?

A duck-filled fatty puss.

"Junior, don't pull the cat's tail."
"I'm only holding it. The cat is pulling it."

What's a tired kangaroo?

Out of bounds.

What do you get when you cross a kangaroo with a snake?

A jump rope.

How do snakes eat so well with no hands?

They have forked tongues.

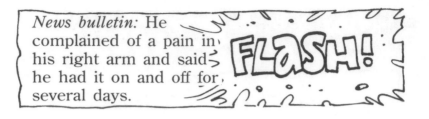

News bulletin: He complained of a pain in his right arm and said he had it on and off for several days.

Why did the girl take a pencil to the shower?
Because she wanted to draw the curtain.

What do you get when you squeeze a curtain?
Drape juice.

What do millionaires eat?
Mints.

What's the best cure for kleptomania?
Klepto-bismol.

What's long, poisonous and tells on you?
A tattlesnake.

How do snakes sign their letters?
Love and hisses.

NA NA NA NA NA NA!...

3. Mind Benders

Where do mummies go for pizza?
Pizza Tut.

MUFFY: Did you hear about the new Dracula doll?
BUFFY: No.
MUFFY: You wind it up and it bites Barbie on the neck.

What kind of coffee does a vampire drink?
De-coffinated.

How do you know when a vampire likes you?
He takes another bite.

What do you call pigs that want everything?
Gimme pigs.

What position does a pig play in baseball?
Short-slop.

What do they put on a criminal pig?
Hamcuffs.

How did they know when the farmer stole the pig?
The pig squealed.

Which are the strongest shellfish on the beach?
Mussels.

WARPED WISE MAN SAYS

Don't go into the water after a big meal. You'll never find it there.

What does a shark use for a barbecue?
Sharkoal.

What happens when a giant meets a shrimp?
He has dinner.

FISH: What's the worst thing about being an octopus?
OCTOPUS: Washing your hands before dinner.

"Why are you crying?"
"I cleaned the bird cage and the canary disappeared."
"How did you clean it?"
"With the vacuum cleaner."

A woman walked into a pet shop having a sale.
"Do you have any birds left?"
The owner told her, "You're in luck. All that twitters is not sold."

What game is played by musicians?
Haydn seek.

What do you call a nervous violin?
High-strung.

What do you call a flutist after he's eaten a lot of candy?
A hyper piper.

"My brother has been playing the guitar for ten years now."
"He must be pretty good."
"Not really. It took him nine years to find out he wasn't supposed to blow through it."

"How can I improve my guitar playing?" asked the student.
"Try playing with the case closed," replied the teacher.

Did you hear about the silly photographer who saved burned-out light bulbs for his darkroom?

"Where did all the rocks on the moon come from?"
"Probably from an ancient comet."
"Where is the comet now?"
"I guess it went back for more rocks."

TEACHER: Can you tell me what kind of rocks are in the Great Lakes?
STUDENT: Wet ones.

What kind of rocks all look alike?
Xerox.

What do they use to clean the Starship Enterprise?
Spock 'n Span.

What's the best way to have a good space party?
Planet.

MAN: Could you give me a ticket for the next trip to the moon?
AGENT: I'm sorry, but the moon is full now.

MOTHER: You know you're not supposed to eat peas with your knife.
JUNIOR: I know, but my fork leaks.

What did one knife say to the other?
"Look sharp."

What kind of killer uses a spoon?
A cereal killer.

How can you tell if an elephant is in your cereal box?
Read the label.

What's a caterpillar?
A worm that's rich enough to buy a fur coat.

What happened when the silkworms had a race?
They ended in a tie.

How do bees get to school?
They take a buzz.

"Ouch! I've just been stung by a bee!"
"Better put something on it."
"Too late. It flew away."

Did you hear about the bird who stuck his beak into a light socket so he could have an electric bill?

Where do birds play baseball?
In the mynah leagues.

What would you get if you crossed a canary with a duck?
A cheep quacker.

"Do you think there is intelligent life on Mars?"
"Sure I do. You don't see them spending billions of dollars to come here, do you?"

TEACHER: Do you know what an echo is?
STUDENT: Could you repeat the question?

TEACHER: Could you tell me about the Iron Age?
STUDENT: I'm sorry. I'm a little rusty on that one.

Why do gorillas have big nostrils?
Because they have big fingers.

What do you call a dumb ape?
Ding Dong.

Why did King Kong cross the road?
To get to Hollywood.

TRAVELLER: I'd like to buy a round-trip ticket, please.
AGENT: To where?
TRAVELLER: Back to here, of course.

TEACHER: Harry, where are the Great Plains?
HARRY: At the great airports.

A flight attendant on an airplane was taking orders. She asked one woman, "Would you like a meal?"
"What are my choices?" asked the woman.
"Yes or no."

What do you call an airplane that flies backwards?
A receding airline.

4. Riddle De De

What's orange and lies on the beach?
A sunburned carrot.

How can you tell when a vegetable is angry?
It's steamed.

"You're early. I told you to come after dinner."
"That's right. That's what I've come after."

What jewelry do vegetables wear?
Onion rings.

CINDY: The recipe says that when the sauce
    starts to boil you should add two teaspoons of
    water.
MINDY: Level or heaping?

What do you call cars in the fall?
Autumn-mobiles.

CUSTOMER: I've come to buy a car, but I don't remember the name. It starts with "T."
CAR SALESMAN: Sorry, we don't have cars that start with tea. All our cars start with gasoline.

TEENAGER: Dad, I have some good news and some bad news.
FATHER: Okay, give me the good news first.
TEENAGER: I drove the car to the supermarket and I'm happy to report that the air bag works great.

"This is a magic car," said the man, as he gave his son the keys.
"Really!" said the teenager.
"Yes," said his father. "One speeding ticket and it will disappear."

Did you hear about the guy who named his car Flattery because it got him nowhere?

Why can't bicycles go as fast as cars?
Because they are two tired.

Two fishermen, Lem and Clem, made a bet on who could catch the first fish. Lem got a bite and was so excited he fell off the pier.
"Hey," said Clem," "if you're going to dive for them, the bet is off."

Why don't fish watch TV?
They don't want to get hooked on it.

What game do baby fish like to play?
Dominnows.

Bud and Bubba rented a boat and fished a lake for several hours. They had a good day and caught over 20 fish. Bud said to Bubba, "Mark this spot so we can come back to it tomorrow."

The next day, when they were going to rent the boat, Bud said, "Did you mark the spot?"

"Yeah," said Bubba. "I put a big X on the side of the boat."

"You fool!" said Bud. "What if we don't get the same boat?"

GAME WARDEN: Didn't you see the sign, NO FISHING ALLOWED?
BOY: That's okay. I'm fishing silently.

What does Tinker Bell use to fry eggs?
A Peter Pan.

"What happened when all the king's men told
Humpty Dumpty a joke?"
"I don't know."
"He fell for it."

Who calls for his pipe, his bowl and his six-pack
of soda?
Old King Cola.

What does a Christmas tree eat with?
Utinsels.

That joke was as funny as poison ivy in a nudist
camp.

What stretches and steals things?
A rubber band-it.

Why was Snow White a good judge?
She was the fairest in the land.

What size soap do judges use?
The trial size.

What kind of parties do prisoners like?
Going-away parties.

JUDGE: You are a habitual criminal. Haven't you ever done anything for anyone else?
DEFENDANT: Well, I kept three or four detectives working regularly.

What do you call a girl with four boyfriends named William?
A Bill collector.

"Your big sister is spoiled, isn't she?"
"No, that's just the perfume she's wearing."

LITTLE ARTHUR: Mom, my sister went and backed the car over my bicycle again.
MOM: Is that right?
BIG SISTER: Yes, but it's his own fault. He shouldn't have left it in the kitchen.

"How come you're wearing your brother's raincoat?"
"I don't want to get his new sweater wet."

DOCTOR: If you sing at the top of your lungs for a half hour every day, you won't be troubled by chest complaints in your old age.

PATIENT: If I do that in my neighborhood, I won't be troubled by old age.

What would you get if you crossed a cold with a leaky faucet?
Cough drops.

What do you put on your feet when you have a cold?
Achoo.

What illness can you catch from a martial arts expert?
Kung flu.

Why do you keep staring at that can of orange juice?

The can says: "Concentrate."

"I got an anonymous letter."
  "From who?"

"You shouldn't play cards with Jim. Don't you know he has a reputation for cheating?"
  "No, he beat me fair and square. He had four aces and I had three."

A young man applied for a summer job.
  "The job," said the employer, "is for a garbage collector. Do you have any experience?"
  "No, sir," said the young man, "but I can pick it up as I go along."

A man was taking a test to be a letter carrier. The first question was: "How far is it from the earth to the moon?"
  "Look," he said, "if that's going to be my route, forget it."

"Looking over your job application, you say you left your last job because of illness."
  "That's right."
  "What kind of illness?"
  "They didn't say. They just told me they were sick of me."

A man filling out a job application came to the part in the form that said: "List the person to notify in case of an emergency."

The man thought and then wrote, "First person you see."

How did the basketball get wet?
The player dribbled it and then dunked it.

WARPED WISE MAN SAYS

Basketball is just a lot of hoopla.

"We just got back from playing a game that came from a tribe in Africa."

"Zulus?"

"No, actually our team won."

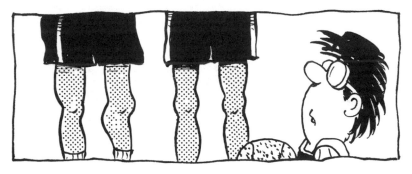

5. Dunce Fever

What do you call a ghost and a zombie that go out on a date?

Boo-friend and ghoul-friend.

What letters do ghosts like to send?

Chain letters.

Why was the invisible man depressed?

He was all dressed up with no face to go.

"Why do monsters have square shoulders?"

"I don't know."

"Because they eat lots of cereal."

"How can cereal give them square shoulders?"

"It's not the cereal. It's the boxes."

Did you hear about the magic dressing room?
When you come out of it you're a changed man.

What do whales chew?
Blubber gum.

What goes, "Ouch, ouch, ouch, ouch. . . . ?"
An octopus with tight shoes.

What do you call sea gulls that live by the bay?
Bagels.

If an athlete gets athlete's foot, what does a
scuba diver get?
Under toe.

What did one cow say to the other cow who was in her way?
"Moovit!"

What happened when the cow jumped over the barbed-wire fence?
Udder disaster.

What gives milk and has two wheels?
A cow on a motorcycle.

What would you get if you crossed a dairy cow with a kangaroo?
I'm not sure, but I think you'd need a pogo stick to milk it.

Show me a finger that's been in Johnson's ear and I'll show you Johnson's wax.

How is food served to the man in the moon?
In satellite dishes.

ASTRONAUT: Captain, we're going faster than the speed of sound.
CAPTAIN: What did you say?

"I just got a job at the space center working the switches."
"Is it a steady job?"
"No, it's sort of on and off."

An alien landed on earth and the first thing he saw was a canary.

"Can you direct me to a hotel?"

"Cheep, cheep," said the bird.

"It better be," replied the alien. "Getting here cost us a fortune."

What birds hang around the ski slopes?
Ski-gulls.

How do robins stay in shape?
They do worm-ups.

What's the best way to get rid of a 100-pound worm in your garden?
Get a 1,000-pound robin.

"What is your hobby?"

"I race pigeons."

"Oh! Have you ever beaten any?"

What do rodents drink in the summer?
Mice tea.

A mother mouse was taking her children for a walk when a large cat jumped at them.

The mother mouse shouted, "Bow-wow!" and the cat ran away.

The mother mouse turned to her children and said, "See, I told you it's good to learn a second language."

Why did the lady mouse want to move?
She was tired of living in a hole in the wall.

What's a mouse's favorite television show?
"Squeal of Fortune."

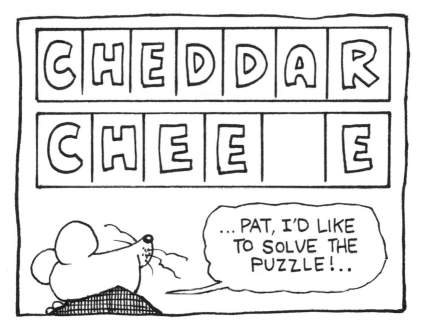

What side dish do miners like to eat?
Coal slaw.

"Why are you eating so fast?"
"I want to eat as much as possible before I lose my appetite."

SCHOOL COOK: All I do is cook, cook, and cook some more! And what do I get for it? Zilch, zero, zip.
STUDENT: Be grateful—we get indigestion.

DEX: Did you hear about the guy who had a helicopter crash?

REX: No, what happened?

DEX: Seems he got cold so he turned off the fan.

What would you get if you crossed an octopus with an ostrich?
Eight dusters.

What would you get if you crossed a cactus with a porcupine?
Sore hands.

What's a caterpillar's worst enemy?
A dog-erpillar.

WARPED WISE MAN SAYS

If the palm of your hand itches, you're going to get something. If your head itches, you've got it.

"You should sing solo."

"Do you really think so?"

"Yes, so low that I can't hear you, and you should sing tenor."

"Really?"

"Absolutely. Ten or so miles away."

"What did you get for your birthday?"

"A harmonica. It's the best present I ever received."

"Why?"

"My mom gives me a dollar a week not to play it."

What do you call a broken phonograph record?
A smash hit.

News bulletin: The orchestra conductor says he has more musicians than he can shake a stick at.

FLASH!

TEACHER: Anyone here quick at picking up music?
STUDENTS: We are.
TEACHER: Great! You two can move the piano.

What do planets like to read?
Comet books.

What's the quickest way for an ant to get to the top of a tree?
The shortest root.

What airplane flies backwards?
An error plane.

GROUND RADAR: Enemy at two o'clock!
PILOT: What should I do till then?

What would you get if you crossed a goat with an eel?
An electric can opener.

6. Teacher's Pests

TEACHER: Edward, you get a "C" on your exam. What does that mean to you?
EDWARD: "Congratulations."

TEACHER: Tell me, when was the Great Depression?
STUDENT: That was when I got my last report card.

TEACHER: Do you thirst after knowledge?
STUDENT: No, I thirst after pretzels.

What tool do you need in math?
Multi-pliers.

What game do horses play?
Stable tennis.

What would you get if you crossed a horse with the house next door?
A nei-ei-ghbor.

RIDING INSTRUCTOR: What kind of saddle do you want on your horse—one with a horn or without?
RIDER: Without. There doesn't seem to be much traffic around here.

What do cowboys put on their pancakes?
Maple stirrup.

"Why do cowboys turn their hats up on the side?"

"I don't know."

"So that three of them can sit in the front in a pickup."

Why do cowboys ride in rodeos?
'Cause they like the extra bucks.

"Doctor, ever since I've been riding in the rodeo, I haven't been feeling good. What do you think it could be?"

"Bronc-itis."

"Doctor, I was playing the flute when I suddenly swallowed it."

"Well, look on the bright side. You could have been playing the piano."

DOCTOR: You have to stop thinking you're a fly.

PATIENT: How do I do that, Doc?

DOCTOR: Well, the first thing is to come down off the ceiling.

"Doctor, you're a genius. You've cured my hearing problem."

"Good. That will be fifty dollars, please."

"What did you say?"

Show me a diet doctor and I'll show you someone who lives off the fat of the land.

Little Audrey asked her mother what the neighbors were going to name the new baby. Her mother told her they were going to name it after her grandmother.

"Won't it be funny," said Little Audrey, "to call a baby 'Grandma'?"

A man rang a doorbell and a little girl came to the door.

"May I speak to your mother?" the man asked the girl.

"She ain't home yet," replied the girl.

"Little girl," he asked her, "where is your grammar?"

"She's upstairs taking a bath."

TOMMY: I learned to count in school today. Listen —one, two, three.

MOTHER: Good. Go on.

TOMMIE: You mean there's more?

PUPIL: Teacher, there's only one pair of boots in the coat room and they're not mine.

TEACHER: Are you sure?

PUPIL: Yes! Mine had snow on them.

What do you get when you drop a letter in the mud?

Blackmail.

"You put too many stamps on that letter."

"Oh, no. Now it will go too far."

At the post office an elderly woman approached another customer and said, "Would you please be kind enough to address this card for me?"

The customer wrote the address and a small note for her.

"Is there anything else I can do for you?" he asked.

"Yes, add at the end: P.S. Please excuse the sloppy handwriting."

TRAFFIC POLICEMAN: This is a ticket for speeding.
DRIVER: Wonderful! When do I get to use it?

Did you hear about the tire that had a nervous breakdown? It couldn't take the pressure.

POLICEMAN: Let me see your license. You were speeding.

DRIVER: But, officer, I was only trying to keep a safe distance between my car and the car in back of me.

Spotting a woman knitting while she was driving, a motorcycle patrolman pulled alongside of her car and shouted, "Pull over!"

"No, silly," said the lady. "It's a pair of mittens."

What has five horns, four wheels and weighs ten tons?
Four rhinos in a convertible.

What would you get if you crossed a jaguar with an elephant?
A sports car with a big trunk.

Why don't elephants play basketball?
Because they don't look good in shorts.

Did you hear about the guy who tried to swim the Atlantic Ocean? He went halfway across and was afraid he wasn't going to make it, so he swam back.

Did you hear the joke about oatmeal? It's a lot of mush.

Did you hear the joke about the firecracker? You'll get a bang out of it.

How do dogs dance in Oz?
On their tippy Totos.

Who brings dogs their presents at Christmas?
Santa Paws.

What kind of dog washes clothes?
A laundermutt.

What kind of market does a dog hate?
A flea market.

"What are the names of your puppies?"
"Rover and Skippy."
"Which one is Rover?"
"The one next to Skippy."

A man got a job painting the white line on the middle of the highway. After three days the foreman called him in to talk with him. "The first day on the job you painted five miles of highway, the second day one mile, and today you only painted 100 feet. How come you're slowing down like that?"

"Can't be helped," replied the man. "I keep getting farther and farther away from the can."

BOY: I'd like to deliver newspapers for your company.
BOSS: Fine. I'll give you three dollars an hour and at the end of the year I'll give you five dollars.
BOY: Okay, I'll come back at the end of the year.

BOSS: Young man, I want you to know that I have a salary increase in mind for you.
YOUNG MAN: That's great! When does it become effective?
BOSS: Just as soon as you do.

News bulletin: The president of the window shade company says he pulls down over 50,000 a year. **FLASH!**

"I'm glad I wasn't born in Spain."
  "Why?"
  "Because I can't speak Spanish."

How many paws does a lion have?
Two, one paw and one maw.

Where does a lion go to exercise?
A jungle gym.

What's a centipede?
An inchworm that converted to the metric system.

What did the girl centipede say to the boy centipede at the dance?
"You're stepping on my foot, my foot, my foot. . . ."

Show me a person with a song in his heart and I'll show you a person with an AM/FM pacemaker.

WARPED WISE MAN SAYS

Time flies like an arrow;
fruit flies like bananas.

What do you call a banana that's been stepped
on?
A banana splat.

How did the peach feel after it was eaten?
Pit-iful.

What do you call a cranberry that eats another
cranberry?
A crannibal.

"Have you heard about the cannibal who loved
fast food?"
"No, what about him?"
"He ordered a pizza with everyone on it."

... I LOVE TO SERVE
MY FELLOW MAN !..

7. Jests For Fun

Why did the cookie go to the doctor?
It was feeling crumby.

"My doctor is slow."
"How slow is he?"
"He's so slow he doesn't have magazines in his waiting room—he has novels."

"Why are you so worried?"
"I lent a guy $3,000 for plastic surgery and now I don't know what he looks like."

"Have you ever seen an oil well?"
"No, but I've never seen a sick one either."

What do you call a rolled-up rabbit?
A hare ball.

What does a rabbit have when it gets a good job offer?
A real hopper-tunity.

What would you get if you crossed a white bear with a rabbit?
A polar hare.

Why do bears have fur?
So their underwear won't show.

What do you call an insect that wears a tuxedo?
A gnatty dresser.

What would you get if you crossed a termite with a praying mantis?
An insect that says grace before eating your house.

On what day do spiders have a good meal?
On flyday.

"On your last fishing trip did you fish with flies?"
"I not only fished with them—I also camped with them, slept with them and ate with them."

Why do hockey players skate on ice?
Because their blades get stuck in the grass.

SOCCER PLAYER: Did you see how close I came to making that goal? I could kick myself for missing it.
TEAMMATE: Don't bother. You'd probably miss.

WARPED WISE MAN SAYS

The reason mountain climbers rope themselves together is to prevent the smart ones from going home.

CITY SLICKER: What do you use that rope for?
COWBOY: To catch cattle.
CITY SLICKER: Oh, really. What do you use for bait?

"Jake, why are you dragging that rope?"
  "Have you ever tried pushing one?"

What did the mother rope say to the baby rope?
  "Don't be knotty."

Why do golfers like Fruit Loops?
  Because there is a hole in every one.

"Playing golf can be bad for your health."
  "What makes you say that?"
  "I just heard a golfer saying he had four strokes on the first hole."

BOOKS NEVER WRITTEN

Personal Hygiene by G.I. Reek

Exploration of the South Pole by I.M. Freeson

How to Get Out of Debt by I.O.A. Bundle

What does a dog say when it gets sick?
"Barf, barf!"
And what does it say when it sits on sandpaper?
"Ruff, ruff!"

How are dogcatchers paid?
By the pound.

"Has your dog a pedigree?"
"Has she! If she could talk, she wouldn't speak to either of us."

What dog bakes cakes?
Betty Cocker.

What did they call Old Macdonald when he joined the Army?
GI, GI, Joe.

What two letters describe the winter?
I C!

DAFFYNITIONS

Dependent clause—one of Santa's helpers.

Conference—meeting of the bored.

Sundial—old timer.

Hatchet—what a hen does to an egg.

Did you hear the joke about the icicle?
It's real cool.

"Great news, son! We've saved enough money to go to Disneyland."
"That's great, Dad. When are we going?"
"As soon as we save enough to get back."

UNCLE: If you're good, I'll give you this bright new penny.
NEPHEW: Haven't you got a dirty old quarter?

TEACHER: Would you please hand me the thesaurus?

BILLY: C'mon, everyone knows the thesaurus became extinct millions of years ago.

TEACHER: Class, close your geography books. Who can tell me where France is?

PUPIL: I know. It's on page 27.

"Have you read any mysteries lately?"
"I'm reading one now."
"What's it called?"
"My math book."

Show me a squirrel's house and I'll show you a nutcracker suite.

Where do owls stay when they take a trip?
At a hoot-el.

What do you call a bird in winter?
A brrrd.

What do you call a frightened woodpecker?
Chicken of the trees.

Why aren't woodpeckers good company?
Because they are always boring.

What did the cloud say to the banker?
"I need a rain check."

What did the cloud have under its raincoat?
Thunderwear.

8. Say What?

Where does smart butter go?
Honor roll.

What's good on bread but bad on the road?
Jam.

How do you make a deer cake?
You use a lot of doe.

Why did the three hammers go to dinner?
They were serving pound cake.

"I finally trained my dog not to beg at the table."
"How did you do that?"
"I let him taste my cooking."

What would you get if you crossed a beagle with a giraffe?
A dog that barks at airplanes.

What would you get if you crossed a pit bull with Lassie?
A dog that bites your leg off and then runs for help.

"I got a slow dog."
  "How can you tell?"
  "This morning he brought me yesterday's newspaper."

"Why are you still standing on that corner? Didn't I tell you to take the 15th Street bus?"
  "Sure, but so far only 10 have gone by."

"I've got good news and bad news. The good news is my father doubled my allowance."
   "What's the bad news?"
   "Two times zero is zero."

"Did I tell you that I had a dream to one day make a million dollars like my father?"
   "Your father made a million dollars?"
   "No, he had the dream too."

"My parents don't understand me. Do yours?"
   "My parents? I don't think they ever met you."

"Are you an only child?"
   "No, I used to be twins."
   "How's that?"
   "My mother says she has a picture of me when I was two."

FATHER: We have twins at our house.
NEIGHBOR: Are they identical?
FATHER: One is and one isn't.

"I married a girl who is a twin."
   "How can you tell them apart?"
   "Her brother has a beard."

"I've come up with the perfect gift for someone who has everything."
   "What is it?"
   "A burglar alarm."

How do they catch crooks at McDonald's?
With burger alarms.

Did you hear about the robbery at the laundromat when two clothespins held up a sheet?

Why did the policeman arrest the young cat?
Because of the kitty litter.

"Did you hear that the police caught a workaholic?"
"What was he charged with?"
"He was resisting a rest."

"I know a guy who stole parts from ten different cars and put them all together."
"What did he get?"
"Twenty years."

A police station received a call: "Someone just stole my truck!"

"Did you see who it was?"

"No, but I got the license number."

DEFENDANT: I'm sorry I took the car, Your Honor.

JUDGE: Why did you take it?

DEFENDANT: It was parked in front of a cemetery and I thought the owner was dead.

DEFENDANT: Judge, I can't be a forger. Why, I can't even write my own name.

JUDGE: You are not accused of writing your own name.

"What happened to your finger?"

"I was trying out my new hammer and hit the wrong nail."

"Are you typing any faster these days?"

"Yep. I'm up to ten mistakes a minute."

How do you praise a computer?

"*Data boy!*"

How did the computers afford a vacation?

They all chipped in.

What happened when they crossed a pit bull with a computer?

Its bark was worse than its megabyte.

POLLY: I was in a new play called *Breakfast in Bed*.

WALLY: Did you have a big role?

POLLY: No, just a little piece of toast with jelly.

RORY: I saw a movie last night on TV called *The Knife Without an Edge*.

LAURIE: How was it?

RORY: Sort of dull.

"Does anyone know what date this is?"

"A copy of the newspaper is on the desk in the other room. Why don't you look it up?"

"Nah, that wouldn't do any good. It's yesterday's paper."

BUCK: I went to a hotel for a change and a rest.

CHUCK: Did you get it?

BUCK: No, the bellboy got the change and the hotel got the rest.

TOURIST: Excuse me. What is this necklace made of?

NATIVE: Alligator teeth.

TOURIST: I guess they have the same value as pearls do to my people.

NATIVE: Not quite. Anyone can open an oyster.

DAD: There is something wrong with my toothbrush.

SON: That's funny. It was all right when I used it to oil my bike chain.

FATHER: Son, why did you let the air out of the tires on your bike?
SON: So I could reach the pedals.

MOTHER: Drink your milk, dear, it makes strong teeth.
LUCY: Why don't you give some to Grandpa?

What do you call a croissant on roller skates?
Breakfast to go.

What does an egg do when another egg bothers it?
Eggnores it.

How do you make a strawberry swirl?
You send it to ballet school.

SANDY: The two things I cook best are apple dumplings and meat loaf.
MANDY: Which is this?

What are unhappy cranberries called?
Blueberries.

Why did the cranberry turn red?
It saw the turkey dressing.

What did the glacier say to the earth?
"Freeze, I've got you covered."

Can polar bears see in a blizzard?
Of course. They have great ice sight.

FARMER: Did the tornado do any damage to your barn, Zeke?

ZEKE: I dunno. I haven't found the doggone thing yet.

What causes the California earthquakes?
I don't know, but it's not San Andreas' Fault.

Why is the sky blue?
Because if it were green, you wouldn't know when to stop mowing the lawn.

TOURIST: Do you make life-size enlargements from snapshots?

PHOTO CLERK: Yes, that's our speciality.

TOURIST: Here are some pictures of the Grand Canyon.

What happened to the guy who got his head stuck in the washing machine?
He got brainwashed.

"In your opinion what is the height of stupidity?"
"How tall are you?"

"Joseph just broke a window."
"How did he do it?"
"I threw a rock at him and he ducked."

"Would you like a knuckle sandwich?"
"No, thanks, but serve yourself."

BOOKS NEVER WRITTEN

What Is Truth? by I. Wonder

I Don't Want It by Yukon Havit

Conceit Can Be Helpful by I.M. Grate

How to Avoid Leaks by Anita Plummer

Faraway Places by I. Ben Dare

Why did the cow want a divorce?
Because she had a bum steer.

What do you call a nervous cow?
Beef jerky.

What did the girl cow say to
the boy cow?
"Let's smooo-ch."

Where do horses stay in a hotel?
In the bridle suite.

Why didn't the horse draw the cart?
He couldn't hold a pencil.

9. Very Punny

What do you call two recently married dandelions?
Newlyweeds.

What do you call a carousel with no brakes?
A merry-go-round and a-round and a-round.

What do you call a window in a palace?
A royal pane.

What do you call a mistake you keep making and that you know you've made before?
A déjà boo-boo.

What do tightrope walkers eat?
A balanced diet.

What do skeletons say before eating?
Bone-appétit.

What's a caveman's favorite place to shop?
Cave Mart.

"I can see into the future."
"When did this start?"
"Next Monday."

"What was the hardest part of preparing
Thanksgiving dinner in prehistoric times?"
"Tell me."
"Stuffing the brontosaurus."

DAFFYNITIONS

Shishkebab—what you say to Kebab when you want him to be quiet.

Out of sight, out of mind— invisible maniac.

Hotel—a place where you pay good dollars for poor quarters.

TEACHER: What are the last words of the Gettysburg Address?
STUDENT: Er—do you mean the zip code?

FATHER: What's the meaning of all these D's and F's on your report card?
SON: That means I'm Doing Fine.

TEACHER: I want you to give me a sentence with an object.
BOY: You are beautiful.
TEACHER: Well, what is the object?
BOY: A good mark.

"I think that if I watch TV for 20 hours every day I will go down in history."
"I'm afraid you'll not only go down in history but also in science, English and math."

Why are you rubbing that food on the back of your sleeve?
They said it was elbow macaroni.

"Waiter, this menu is blank on one side."
"That's in case you're not hungry."

"Boy, this food is really terrible," said the diner.
"Gee," said the waiter. "Anything else wrong?"
"Yeah," said the customer, "the portions are too small."

TOM SWIFTIES

"I dropped my toothpaste," said Tom, crestfallen.

"Archery is such an aimless sport," said Tom with a quiver.

"This horse won't stop," said Tom woefully.

"The whole thing sounds like a fairy tale," Tom said grimly.

"Why are the letters 'B' and 'Y' so important?"
"I don't know."
"Because we couldn't get 'by' without them."

JIM: I have a friend who doesn't know the
meaning of the word "fear."
KIM: That so?
JIM: Yes, he's afraid to ask.

What is confidence?
*Confidence is going after Moby Dick in a
rowboat with a pea-shooter and a jar of tartar
sauce.*

What is the most famous skunk statue in Egypt?
The Stinx.

What does a skunk do before going to school?
Puts on its stinking cap.

Did you hear the joke about the banana peel? It slips my mind.

What's green with red spots?
A pickle with chicken pox.

What's black and white and green?
A seasick penguin.

What's black and white and pink all over?
A pig in a tuxedo.

...A FINE-LOOKING SWINE!

Where do pigs like to sit?
On pork benches.

What do you call a pig that takes acting lessons?
A hamateur.

BOOKS NEVER WRITTEN

Inside a Garbage Truck by Howie Volting

Fact or Fiction? by Izzy Lyon

Weight Lifting by Buster Gutt

How to Improve Your Teeth by Floss M. Moore

Show me a person who sleeps through a long speech and I'll show you a bulldozer.

What was the nearsighted chicken doing in the billiard parlor?
Trying to hatch the cue ball.

What did the chicken say when she laid a square egg?
"Ouch!"

What are goose bumps for?
To keep geese from speeding.

What happened when the boy snake and the girl snake got into an argument?
They hissed and made up.

Why did the clock get kicked out of school?
Because it was tocking.

TEACHER: Why are you late for school?
STUDENT: I couldn't help it. School started before I got here.

"Let's play school."
"Well, okay. But let's pretend I'm absent."

TEACHER: Please answer when I call your name—John Martin.
BILLY: Absent.
TEACHER: Please, Billy, let John answer for himself.

"My teacher said I could do anything I wanted at recess."
"What did you do?"
"I went home."

News bulletin: The librarian's convention was booked solid. **FLASH!**

PRINCIPAL: Young man, you are different from the rest of the class.
YOUNG MAN: Really?
PRINCIPAL: Yes, they're graduating.

10. Stay After School Specials

What's worse than being a two-ton witch?
Being her broom.

What do little ghosts prefer to frisbees?
Boo-merangs.

How do dentists fix dragon teeth?
With a fire drill.

What's green and makes holes?
A drill pickle.

What cheese do people live in?
Cottage cheese.

"I don't like the cheese with the holes in it."
"Then just eat the cheese and leave the holes on your plate."

CUSTOMER: What dressing do you have for the salad?
WAITER: Blue cheese.
CUSTOMER: What other colors have you got?

What do you call a whale that talks a lot?
A blubbermouth.

Where does Albert Einstein keep his fish?
In a think tank.

What do you call a rabbit that is owned by a beetle?
A bug's bunny.

What do you call a chubby jack-o'-lantern?
A plumpkin.

What do you call four bullfighters in quicksand?
Quatro cinco.

Why aren't robots ever afraid?
They have nerves of steel.

Do robots have brothers?
No, they have transistors.

A plumber went to the house of a customer.
"I'm sorry I'm a few days late to fix the leak in your basement," the plumber said.
"Oh," replied the wet customer, "the time wasn't totally wasted. Since I called you, I taught my daughter to swim."

What happens when a Finnish swimmer gets into trouble?
Helsinki.

"Did you hear they found the gene for shyness?"
"No, I wonder why they didn't find it before?"
"It was hiding behind some other genes."

"I slept with my head under the pillow last night."

"What happened?"

"The tooth fairy came and took my teeth out."

"I tried to keep my waterbed a secret."

"What happened?"

"It leaked out."

What do cows read in the morning?

The moos-paper.

What do mangos like to read?

Mango-zines.

FATHER: Why didn't you bring your books home?

LITTLE ALICE: Dad, they're school books, not home books.

Did you hear about the queen who threatened to hang the court jester if he didn't collect the morning mist in a bottle? It was a question of dew or die.

WARPED WISE MAN SAYS

You know it's time to worry when a call goes out for two of all the animals to be sent to Cape Canaveral.

What did the little pine tree say to the big pine tree?

"*Stop needling me.*"

What organized gang destroys wool coats?
The mothia.

LAWYER: So you say the defendant has a habit of talking to himself when he's alone.

WITNESS: That's hard to say—I've never been with him when he's alone.

"Which amendment gives you the right to pull up your sleeves?"

"I don't know."

"The Second Amendment—the right to bare arms."

What superhero doesn't like to share things?
Bratman.

What kind of soda do Australian bears drink?
Coca-koala.

What's red, white and blue?
A sad candy cane.

What would you get if you dropped an ice cream on the floor?
A plopsicle.

What would you get if you crossed chocolate pudding with your mother's high-heeled shoes?
Yelled at.

Did you hear about the lawn mower that got tired of being pushed around?

What is the loneliest place in Louisiana?
Bayou self.

What does an alligator sing?
Scales.

"That guy over there is the laziest person I've ever seen. He's done nothing but sit on that park bench for three hours."
"How do you know that?"
"I've been sitting here and watching him the whole time."

SUNDAY SCHOOL TEACHER: Which parable do you like best?
WILLIE: The one about the multitude that loafs and fishes.

What do you want to be when you grow up?
Taller.

How do you measure poison ivy?
By itches.

How did the magician make the blackboard disappear?
Slate of hand.

"I'd like to buy a pair of thermal underwear."
"How long do you want them?"
"From October to March."

"Why don't you wash your neck?"
"Then it wouldn't match my sneakers."

"Which three ways do men wear their hair?"
"How?"
"Parted, unparted and departed."

"Did you hear about the woman who put too much mousse on her hair?"
"No, what happened?"
"She grew antlers."

TOM SWIFTIES

"I may trim the shrub," Tom hedged.

"I don't like volcanoes," Tom erupted.

"I touched a live wire," said Tom glowingly.

"This is the end," Tom concluded.

About the Author

Charles Keller has been working and playing with comedy all his life. Working for CBS as a script consultant, he edited many of the great classic sit-coms, such as *M*A*S*H, All in the Family,* and the *Mary Tyler Moore Show,* and he also worked on other prime-time comedy programs. He got started writing children's books because he didn't like many of the ones he read and thought he could do better. Now, over 40 books later, he maintains the country's largest archive of children's rhymes, riddles, witty sayings and jokes, constantly updating his massive collection. When he isn't writing children's books, he can be found creating educational software computer programs for children. Born in New York, Charles Keller is a graduate of St. Peter's College. He presently resides in Union City, New Jersey.

About the Illustrator

Jeff Sinclair has been drawing cartoons ever since he could hold a pen. He has won several local and national awards for cartooning and humorous illustration. When he is not at his drawing board, he can be found renovating his home and working on a water garden in his backyard. Jeff has recently gone into cyberspace on the Internet. He lives in Vancouver, British Columbia, in Canada, with his wife Karen, son Brennan, daughter Conner, and golden lab Molly.

Index

THE END!!